LOOK WE HAVE COMING TO DOVER!

Look We Have Coming to Dover!

DALJIT NAGRA

faber and faber

First published in 2007
by Faber and Faber Limited
3 Queen Square London WC1N 3AU

Typeset by Faber and Faber Ltd
Printed in England by T. J. International Ltd, Padstow, Cornwall

A CIP record for this book
is available from the British Library

ISBN 978-0-571-23122-5

GIFT

10 9 8 7 6 5 4 3

The people have brown faces – besides, there are so
many of them! Are they really the same flesh as yourself?
Do they even have names? Or are they merely a kind of
undifferentiated brown stuff . . .

— GEORGE ORWELL

Acknowledgements

Versions of these poems appeared in the following publications:

Forward Book of Poetry 2005 (Forward Press, 2004); *Guardian*; *New Writing 10* (Picador, 2001); *Oh My Rub!* (Smith/Doorstop Books, 2003); *Poetry London*; *Poetry Review*; *Redbeck Anthology of British South Asian Poetry* (Redbeck, 2000); *Rialto*; *Soundings*; *Stand*; *Wasafiri*.

Thanks are due to: Babel – Literature & Talks, Royal Festival Hall in association with Apples & Snakes; the Royal Society of Medicine in association with the Calouste Gulbenkian Foundation; the Arts Council England for a First Verse Award.

Additional thanks are due to Matthew Hollis and Paul Keegan for their editorial comments, to Katherine Hoyle for her insights, and to Stephen Knight for being the perfect mentor who has inspired and guided me over the years.

I would also like to thank my brother Daljinder, my friends Steve and Neil, and Escha – my wonderful daughter!

Contents

LOOK WE HAVE COMING TO DOVER!

Darling & Me!

Di barman's bell done dinging
        so I phone di dimply-mississ,
Putting some gas on cookah,
        bonus pay I bringin!

Downing drink, I giddily
        home for Pakeezah record
to which we go-go, tango,
        for roti – to kitchen – she rumba!

I tell her of poor Jimmy John,
        in apron his girlfriend
she bring to pub his plate of
        chicken pie and dry white

potato! Like Hilda Ogden,
        Heeya, eaht yor chuffy dinnaaah!
She huffing off di stage
        as he tinkle his glass of Guinness.

We say we could never eat
        in publicity like dat, if we did
wife advertisement may need
        of solo punch in di smack.

I pull her to me – my skating
        hands on her back are Bolero
by Torvill and Dean. Giggling
        with bhangra arms in air

she falling for lino, till I
       swing her up in forearm!
Darling is so pirouettey with us
       for whirlwind married month,

that every night, though by day
       we work factory-hard, she always
have disco of drumstick in pot.
       Hot. Waiting for me.

A Prelude to Suka's Adventures
from the Board Room

He was the first from our farms on a cheap boat ride to Britain.
Within a year of work, showered
with overtime, he sent home his pounds for an Enfield bike.
Dripping in black and silver
it posed in the courtyard. Our scooters farting on the parched
soil as we left-behinds would meet
to be drawn by the pull from the flood of his letters that swore
on swift returns for a small price.

I crossed the sea, like those Englishmen who made their names
abroad,
for his damp and graffiti'd house
where he threw up a panel of chip wood on the bath, and titled
this my bedroom. Whispering
there's a stream of shift-working men, sleeping days or nights,
swamping the shared space.
Then he sucked the chain on his steaming piss. In the kitchen
he fed me cardboard chapattis.

I had left my wife, and the drip of mail from wherever
at my village postal job,
for this once always-drunk, street-sweeper's boy made good.
When I asked about the button-
pushing work he'd gushingly written of, I almost choked
at his head on a body of stick,
at the ash of ghostly hair and the sunken eyes
as he laughed and laughed through his yellow teeth.

Booking Khan Singh Kumar

Must I wear only masks that don't sit for a Brit
Would you blush if I stripped from my native skin

Should I beat on my chest I'm a ghetto poet
Who discorded his kind as they couldn't know it

Should I foot it featly as a Punjab in Punglish
Sold on an island wrecked by the British

Did *you* make me for the gap in the market
Did *I* make me for the gap in the market

Does it feel good in the gap in the market
Does it feel gooey in the gap in the market . . .

Will I flame on the tree that your canon has stoked
Will I thistle at the bole where a bull-dog cocked

Should I talk with the chalk of my white inside
On the board of my minstrel – blacked outside

Should I bleach my bile-name or mash it to a stink
Should I read for you straight or Gunga Din this gig

Did *you* make me for the gap in the market
Did *I* make me for the gap in the market

Do I need to be good in the gap in the market
Do I need to be gooey in the gap in the market . . .

As I've worn a sari bride and an English Rose
Can I cream off awards from your melting-pot phase

Do you medal yourselves when you meddle with my type
If I go up di spectrum how far can ju dye

More than your shell-like, your clack applause
What bothers is whether you'll boo me if I balls

Out of Indian!

For the Wealth of India

'I mean to cut a channel . . . that men might quickly sail to India.'
– CHRISTOPHER MARLOWE, *Tamburlaine*

To Aeroflot the savage miles
in a moment, tucking under
continents to clip the distance,
zoomed to our ancestral homeland
so we ransack the bazaar tracks
of back-alley bounteous Jullunder,
ranting down the marker-prices
to a smudge paid by my permed
aunty in Walsall, bombing
through the brightly lit boutiques,
mum beating a brow, stomping
a finger so a gold-toothed owner
clicks to a knobbly-knees, bent-neck
man who trays us with milky sweets
and cans of Fanta, who says,
God you bless Memsahibs! –
twisting away with a snarl, I see it,
punting my heel up his arse
I scurry him off like a rat!

From the stools of the shop, postered
with Madhuri Dixit and Wham!
we shoot through the glossy pages
of the tea-stained catalogues
for the blood-sari to wow the guests
into awe when I walk the aisle
to the Holy Book of my biggest day.
That's the style mummy!
I need it now mummy!

The ultimate design to highlight
my super-long legs, but the tailors
scratch their necks, snort,
reversing some phlegm until mum
clears them with her finest English:
Vut is dis corruption? Vee
need it fut-a-fut, or must vee
go to the clean-nosed Hindu
with cut-cut scissors, next door?
Daddy would applaud if he wasn't
slogging at the concrete factory.

The pongy tailors run like flies
now that time is against them
as we debate with the queue of Englanders
the top-carat beauty of exotic
things, and which riff-raff road
in Southall we all left for Harrow,
the locals steal looks from us for ages
until mum blinks them with the sun
off her gemmed Rolex, I wonder
if mum's old family were trapped
over here, too sweaty for style
with all the pig-sniffing sewers
so heavy and holding, ah well
what a shame, as we lap up
our suits, shoes and bags
of bangles and cheapo knickers
tossing them at the slouched driver
of the flimsy rickshaw to shout,
Jaldi! Jaldi! Back to Britain!
Get us out of here! – spinning
a penny to some limbless in a bucket.

Sajid Naqvi

After we found our friend spread in his student room in Neasden,
overtaken by a freak heart attack, we were cordially invited
to the mosque. All the relatives who'd come flying out
of the woodwork packaged him into white cotton garments,
the kind they all wore as they stiffed straight past us.

They'd oiled and patted his hair, dismantled the grungy look
which had gone with his black clothes. His face was varnished
into glazed fruit and put on display. He'd sit nocturnally
crunching his way through Maths equations with The Smiths.
Instead, someone croaked endless hymns from the Koran.

His divorced mother was forbidden by custom to show up
so his father from Derby was there to bring him in line
and give him a fitting ending. He helped to seal the lid,
load him on. We shadowed the hearse outward through narrow
roads, winding up in deepest Surrey, at a Shi'ite cemetery

where the prayers raged again, chanting over his lowered
coffin, hitting the box with the force of the hard soil
his family threw, as they tucked away our Saj.

Yobbos!

The first step towards lightening THE WHITE MAN's *burden
is through teaching the virtues of cleanliness.*
– Pears Soap advert, 1899

A right savage I was – sozzled
to the nose with sprightly
Muldoon, squeezed into the communal

sweat of a Saturday tube home –
I'm up to p. 388 of his sharp lemon-skinned
Collected Poems

when some scruffy looking git pipes to his crew –
*Some Paki shit, like,
eee's loookin into!*

My blood rising, especially when my head's
done in with words like
'Badhbh' . . . 'Cailidin' . . . 'Salah-eh-din',

I nearly get blunt, as one of them –
*Well mate, this Paki's more British than that inde-
cipherable, impossibly untranslatable*

sod of a Paddy –
only I don't 'cos I catch my throat gungeing
on its Cromwellian vile, my tongue foaming for soap . . .

Our Town with the Whole of India!

Our town in England with the whole of India sundering
out of its temples, mandirs and mosques for the customised
streets. Our parade, clad in cloak-orange with banners
and tridents, chanting from station to station for Vasaikhi
over Easter. Our full-moon madness for Eidh with free
pavement tandooris and legless dancing to boostered
cars. Our Guy Fawkes' Diwali – a kingdom of rockets
for the Odysseus-trials of Rama who arrowed the jungle
foe to re-palace the Penelope-faith of his Sita.

Our Sunrise Radio with its lip sync of Bollywood lovers
pumping through the rows of emporium cubby holes
whilst bhangra beats slam where the hagglers roar
at the pulled-up back-of-the-lorry cut-price stalls.
Sitar shimmerings drip down the furbishly columned
gold store. Askance is the peaceful Pizza Hut . . .
A Somali cab joint, been there for ever, with smiley
guitar licks where reggae played before Caribbeans
disappeared, where years before Teddy Boys jived.

Our cafés with the brickwork trays of saffron sweets,
brass woks frying flamingo-pink syrup-tunnelled
jalebis networking crustily into their familied clumps.
Reveries of incense scent the beefless counter where
bloodied men sling out skinned legs and breasts
into thin bags topped with the proof of giblets.
Stepped road displays – chock-full of ripe karela,
okra, aubergine – sunshined with mango, pineapple,
lychee. Factory walkers prayer-toss the river of

sponging swans with chapattis. A posse brightens
on park-shots of Bacardi – waxing for the bronze
eyeful of girls. The girls slim their skirts after college
blowing dreams into pink bubble gums at neck-
descending and tight-neck sari-mannequins. Their grannies
point for poled yards of silk for own-made styles.
The mother of the runaway daughter, in the marriage
bureau, weeps over the plush-back catalogues glossed
with tuxedo-boys from the whole of our India!

X

i knot my tongue
i nail my lips
i zip my lids

       & still   u say
          i say   u harm

u hook my arms
u hood my head
u lose my legs

       & still   u say
          i say   u harm

The Man Who Would be English!

Just for kicks I was well in with the English race,
my skin matched the beef of their ruddy skin
as one by one a walk-in sing-along of familiar faces
from the lark-about days of school chucked back chunks
of smoke to reveal their manhood, I shouldered the bulk
as they broadened like brick houses to broadly take me in,
we plundered up gulps of golden rounds for the great game,
united at our local, we booed at the mounted screen –
at the face of the anthem'd foreigner when we were at home.
Then we chanted with heart and soul for God and Queen!

I was one of us, at ease, so long as I passed
my voice into theirs – I didn't *bud-bud ding-ding*
on myself for dropping the asylum side to sign up
for the bigger picture. I wasn't Black or Latin or managed
by a turbaned ghost. No distant land forever
with rights to my name . . . At an own goal, I pitched up,
caught my mother on the screen, as keeper, in our net
gloving the ball with lard, from the Mutiny, launching it
into my hands, ticking, at the end of the day, as I walked alone
to my wife – outside on a sideline of frost, kicking off:

D-d-doze err shrubby peeepalll . . . !!!
D-d-deyy sprayyy all um ourrr valll . . . !!!
Venn hmmm veee g-go bbackkk . . . !!!
Lookk lookk ju nott British ju rrr blackkk . . . !!!

Bibi & the Street Car Wife!

O son, I widow each day by netted windows
playing back days when my daughter-in-law
hooting over hot sands with chapel-less feet
would basket her head on fields of live carrot,
then cowed by courtyard wall with peacock sari
and mousy head, she would mould me dung
buns in caramel sun to pass our village audition.

Her boogly eyes would catch my fast grip ripping
the shokri hairstyle of each carrot, potting
the pan for Indian skinning the slices, tossing under
her buns to drama the screen of fire, *Don't watch it –*
water the carrots for sauce! Directing our fresh
bride, so like Madhur Jaffrey on telly
she soak my applause on praise of stuffing husband.

Ever since we loosened our village acres
for this flighty mix-up country, like moody
actress she buy herself a Datsun, with legs
of KFC microphoning her mouth
(ladies of temple giddily tell me her tale):
she manicured waves men, or honking horn
to unbutton her hair she dirty winking:
Come on friend, I like it letting you in!

What to make of wife who hawking late
from Terminal Two to bad blood me: *We*
no needing this car-park house you share,
in your name, clamping us to back-seat

of your cinema. In 'my' movie, old lady,
I meat you for boot of my Turkmenistani
departure! She propeller her fist
with drumstick, in landing light, then bite!

Beef-burgering her backside on our 5Ks,
what do we care for the toilet of her big
bank balance? O son, as you wheel the taco
meter of your lorry for days then sofa to me
as now, who does she her black-box film
shoot with to blow 'our' soaring name?
O my only son, why will she not lie down
for us, to part herself, to drive out babies?

In a White Town

She never looked like other boys' mums.
No one ever looked without looking again
at the pink kameez and balloon'd bottoms,

mustard-oiled trail of hair, brocaded pink
sandals and the smell of curry. That's why
I'd bin the letters about Parents' Evenings,

why I'd police the noise of her holy songs,
check the net curtains were hugging the edges,
lavender-spray the hallway when someone knocked,

pluck all the gold-top milk from its crate
in case the mickey-takers would later disclose it,
never confessing my parents' weird names

or the code of our address when I was licked
by Skinheads (by a toilet seat)
desperate to flush out the enemy within.

I would have felt more at home had she hidden
that illiterate body, bumping noisily into women
at the market, bulging into its drama'd gossip,

for homework – in the public library with my mates,
she'd call, scratching on the windows. Scratching again
until later, her red face would be in my red face,

two of us alone, she'd duck at my stuttered Punjabi,
laughing, she'd say I was a gora, I'd only be freed
by a bride from India who would double as her saathi.

Nowadays, when I visit, when she hovers upward,
hobbling towards me to kiss my forehead
as she once used to, I wish I could fall forward.

Arranged Marriage

My mum cramming a globe of ladoo
against the will of my gob.
Flushing it through thanks to the slick
of syrup. There, in the cramped
moist temple, on cue, she oozed
from her crocodile purse a wad

of firmed notes – circling their halos
for ages over my head
for the ceremony with video crew.
Dropped her load. Then dropped
again for the cross-legged bride.
Emptied, she bowed to her god.

Granny hobbled out a ladoo
and crashed it home with prune
fingers – the mash of their beads
on my gritted teeth, a feast
for flies, as the preacher chorused
the whole hush-temple rose.

Zombying behind both me and the bride,
each fixed pose was frozen in line,
moth-ball scented, a twenty-twenty
video vision of ponies, monkeys
floated in turns by wedlocked pairs.
Soft the parting that bullioned the air.

Numb, I sat
a costumed prat
as the cash bedded
I deadened my head
from holy muzak
(and *buk-buk-buk*
still feeling sick
started to let rip

necklaced in flowers,
from another world,
between my lap
inside the turban
of moaning harmonium
that bored me rigid),
when my deaf grandad
in fake posh-Indian:

Who says today's children don't eat the old food?
Did you see how my boy has stuffed his ladoos?

Parade's End

Dad parked our Granada, champagne-gold
by our superstore on Blackstock Road,
my brother's eyes scanning the men
who scraped the pavement frost to the dole,
one 'got on his bike' over the hill
or the few who warmed us a thumbs-up
for the polished recovery of our re-sprayed car.

Council mums at our meat display
nestled against a pane with white trays
swilling kidneys, liver and a sandy block
of corned beef, loud enough about the way
darkies from down south *Come op ta*
Yorksha, mekkin claaims on aut theh can
befoh buggrin off in theh flash caahs!

At nine, we left the emptied till open,
clicked the dials of the safe. Bolted
two metal bars across the back door
(with a new lock). Spread trolleys
at ends of the darkened aisles. Then we pressed
the code for the caged alarm and rushed
the precinct to check it was throbbing red.

Thundering down the graffiti of shutters
against the valley of high-rise flats.
Ready for the getaway to our cul-de-sac'd
semi-detached, until we stood stock-still:
watching the car-skin pucker, bubbling smarts
of acid. In the unstoppable pub-roar
from the John O'Gaunt across the forecourt,

we returned up to the shop, lifted a shutter,
queued at the sink, walked down again.
Three of us, each carrying pans of cold water.
Then we swept away the bonnet-leaves
from gold to the brown of our former colour.

On the Birth of a Daughter

It wasn't that I found out
on the day you were released,
your mother's subterfuge
in coming off the pill.
It wasn't that our parents
egged her on
to keep me hitched.
It wasn't that you
were so late you were
nearly punch-drunk
or stillborn.
Or all that epidural
from your bubble
bursting you
for the hornet's nest
of hairs – that curtain
through which
you were staged
reeking of scatol, scotch.
Nor was it your full black
woman's lips, flushed
like a fresh cut, that pushed me
nose on to grief and joy. Or
your slant oriental eyes – blind
to the forced marriage
drawing you in.
It was simply this:
you didn't look like us.

You looked for all the world
that you'd almost pass
for anybody's baby.
I loved you for your genetic slip
from our messy family business.
As you cried in my arms,
I delivered you up to your mum
who held you
              against herself.

The Speaking of Bagwinder Singh Sagoo!

Why now not be naked, you naughty western woman?
Not four month since I Delhi–Heathrow to you,
already you lying in living room with catalogues
of Bombay passions, rolling into my praying father
to give him cardigan arrest! Mother still have her trunk
of dowry, each year from it she stitch a shiny couture'd
salwaar in minutes, and no one notice she stand out.
But your tightening of the dowry of the costume bottoms
is a punky drain-piping! Not *we* made for upping
cardboard base so ankle flashing, but *we* for baggy,
we for smiley wide-pride of pyjama leg,
puckered by you into bony lady's bellybutton!

Our peoples at the Sugar Puff factory, I overhear
poison their wives at night monster their heads
crazy with: *She was in film-star red*, one says.
No, no, another replies, *she's in chocolate sauce.*
The sweaty-necked boiler-suit boy, chicken-dancing,
even louder: *No, no, no, I saw her at market*
with milky teeth, in the company of her doctor –
the Avon Lady. I swear by all the gods in my locker
she was in the Dulux of British poodle pink!
They toss up their chapatti rolls, their Black Jack cards,
in this break for lunch – only at your toenails.
I make up constipation for shame of leaving the loo!

Turn off those sunglasses. Is it summer in this evening
of winter? Look at me, what is that cherry jelly
lumping the lash of your eyes? Are you bleeding upwards?

Those mascara scars? This half cut hair-mop?
How can this be a forehead for the special red bindi
when it's undressed by dirty-love bride (from college!)
who tie my arms with jockstraps from my B-team
hockey days. All night long – the pouncing, the tickling,
the lipstick and 'odour toilet'. My father blowing a cough
as you put my bottom up my backside! I cannot meditate,
pray, lock into my lotus position! I cannot close my legs!
Oh my Rub, what is England happening for us?

8

If someone had said you passed away
this evening at 8, when my watch was still
an hour behind, on a few minutes to seven,
I'd be round for rituals with your loved ones.
We'd sip the last of your lemon tea, taking
turns to embrace you with private words.
Some would simply freeze you
with that wholly unsayable look of love.

In the quickening, we'd fold away your clothes,
close the curtains over the awful pouring
light, but couldn't do a thing for the beep
& brake of cars, the low hum of a fast
travelling bus as we'd help you to the awkward
angle on your bed, how you'd be found,
then we'd hold back for the aweful way you'd rise
to the almighty challenge of your punctual

heart-stop.

        Making our journeys home
        we were back in time
        strangely prepared
        when someone said
        you passed away
        this evening at 8.

The Tree

The tree my father grew
from his garden I take an axe

and branch by branch
I break the tree

and set to work
the million maddened bits,

the fire of night.
Only for ash I keep.

Rapinder Slips into Tongues . . .

Dad and me were watching the video –
Amar, Akbar, Anthony. It's about three
brothers separated after the family is parted
by gangsters. You can get it with subtitles, Miss.
When Anthony, who grows up in a Catholic home,
begged Christ for the address of his real parents
then crossed himself, I jumped off our royal red
sofa, joined Anthony with his prayer:
Hail Mary, Hail Mary, Hail Mary,
four-quartering myself then curtseying a little.

Dad just stared at me, knocking his turban side
to side that I almost thought it would come off
which it normally does when he's doing his press-ups
and his face goes mauve. Instead he took off
his flip-flop (the one with a broken thong),
held it in the air, shouting in 'our' language:
Vut idiot! If you vunt to call on Gud,
call anytime on anyvun of our ten gurus.
Do yoo tink is white Gud's wife yor mudder?

Dad's got a seriously funny way Miss,
sometimes he cries, and says he's going to give me
to a Sikh school, a proper school. That's why
I did what my cousin Ashok does at our local
temple – while you were all doing Hail Mary
to end registration, I first locked my hands,
knelt down, prayed with this ditty we do on Sundays,

imagined the Golden Temple and our bearded gods
to your up-on-the-cross one, then roared:
Wahay Guru!
Wahay Guru!
Wahay Guru!
Like that.

Look We Have Coming to Dover!

'So various, so beautiful, so new . . .'
– MATTHEW ARNOLD, 'Dover Beach'

Stowed in the sea to invade
the alfresco lash of a diesel-breeze
ratcheting speed into the tide, brunt with
gobfuls of surf phlegmed by cushy come-and-go
tourists prow'd on the cruisers, lording the ministered waves.

Seagull and shoal life
vexing their blarnies upon our huddled
camouflage past the vast crumble of scummed
cliffs, scramming on mulch as thunder unbladders
yobbish rain and wind on our escape hutched in a Bedford van.

Seasons or years we reap
inland, unclocked by the national eye
or stabs in the back, teemed for breathing
sweeps of grass through the whistling asthma of parks,
burdened, ennobled – poling sparks across pylon and pylon.

Swarms of us, grafting in
the black within shot of the moon's
spotlight, banking on the miracle of sun –
span its rainbow, passport us to life. Only then
can it be human to hoick ourselves, bare-faced for the clear.

Imagine my love and I,
our sundry others, Blair'd in the cash
of our beeswax'd cars, our crash clothes, free,
we raise our charged glasses over unparasol'd tables
East, babbling our lingoes, flecked by the chalk of Britannia!

Journey

There you go
with your rucksack of clean clothes
and a flat rose in your notepad
wandering for the dream you had
where all the things you spilled
were back in their bottles, brighter
than ever . . .

Karela!

for Katherine

Gourd, grenade-shaped,
okra-green. I prise
each limb of warty flesh,
disembowel each indi-
gestible red-seed memory
of regal pomegranate.
This dish from my past, I recall
mum would embalm the innards
with amalgam of fried onion
to gum the snarled temper.
Mummy-bound with string
for a mustard-popping pan.
Then sealed. Masala creeps . . .

Karela, ancient as crocodile,
no matter I kiln-crisp
each skin for ages, proudly
before my English lover,
when the lid comes off
each riven body shrivelled
yet knurl-fisted and gnarled –
blackening centuries of heat
with a feedback of sizzling
smoke and wog – rescinders
stoking my mind with inedible
historical fry-ups. The rebel
ethic of our ethnic gumbo!

Hail to the King of Bile
as I bite a mean mouthful
swamping me down to the tracts
of my roots – my body craves
taste of home but is scolded
by shame of blood-desertion
(that simmers in me unspoken),
save that we are in love –
that you bite as well your mind
with karela-curses, requited
knowledge before our seed
can truly bloom, before
our tongue is pure poppy!

The Furtherance of Mr Bulram's Education

How to unearth a position as English Teacher when our Indians
are drowning Bacardis to bawdy din in darkling gardens.
Early to rise, they gaudy our cul-de-sacs
with pink turbans, cardamom breath
singing away for work,
as their offspring
en route
to comprehensives:
pea-shooting through hedges
at the squirrels on our bird-house. Must all
of us be tarred when we spring from murmuring streams
that winged on songs of cuckoo and dove to our Hill Station
study where our métier was mastering the diction of Dr Johnson,
the Homeric canon,
for our vocation calling,
our trophy:
the remnant Auburns of Albion.

So observe our Albion as they hotchpotch the hortus of their Edwardian
homes by smuggling 'cousins' into the shed as spare room,
by gouging the path fringes for coriander,
by mounting soil with steamingly sour
manure before they spew it,
ruck it for
the industrial
production of swede,
cabbage, carrot, turnip.
Trees survive the hired chainsaw
if they are apple, plum or pear bearing.
Nothing is for looking at per se when the patio is pickles,
when the earth's uprooted by their anthem of drills, when the rear
six foot wall is crowned
with the infantry of cracked
glass in cement,
to fortress their sceptred isles.

And today, Mrs Bulram, one of these onion-breath Calibans clattered
his shovel on stones where our fence is lowest, then shook
my hand, hoisted two chafed fingers as squealing
shears – beheading the shivering privet
between us. He's plotting
aloos to carpe
diem
with our roses.
Vut? Dis fancy pots?
Dat's a gora potiness!
We dig dis body! We grow faster!
His rash Punjabi, as he stretched his farmer's
arm around my blazer, *Da Crown in India only ju wear.*
Here dey dirt ju brudder.
Tonight, my wife and cousins –
you plant us Queen's
quick 'shop-keeper' English!!!

Digging

Squatted against the bedroom door with left leg
stretched, wiping sweat from my thigh,
I shave hairs to the shape of a passport photo.
Into the good skin, steeling along
the top end of the picture – a straight incision
until blob by seamless blob, over
the Stanley knife, a rivering of blood.

Once under the fold, down to the roots,
nerve-hand holds for slicing
level the parallel lines of a photo.
Leaning deeper so the unconscious,
deeper so the gore geometric be heaped up,
I drop the silvery haft, the leg,
lug back the flap.

I hear a cry from some of myself.
So this is me. This
jameen. This meat
for which I war
myself.
This.

Jaswinder Wishes it was Easy Being Black

Mum has me reared up tall
like I'm posed for a marriage
market, same as the necklaced
cow flapping our calendar
she makes me sheep my eyes,
shelled in salwaar once hers.
My Miss Dynamite strut
brings out the wag of her finger
as I servant chai and mum's
'famed' Bombay Mix
to sofas of ogling visitors
who feed on me their gobs.

Ms Victory, my English teacher,
in a voice like Maya Angelou or Toni Morrison
that she plays us with head high,
she asked us to write our imaginary homes –
our mud hut back home I can't magic-eye
so much as my house as a tucked-away
country where sorted women get a life!

Sometimes I wish I was a black woman.
Black women are chilled, get the space like white women.
Ms Victory chats English with everyone she knows.
Ms Victory from work splits for herself.
Ms Victory, *nuh uh*, she don't do shame.
Ms Victory goes clubbing. Ms Victory rules
the ball and spins them howling lyrics on their heart-
broken phones. Ms Victory cabs her rip-tight gear
and red lips through homelands of London for the island of her

home. Ms Victory is a flag of freedom.
Ms Victory spills her heels to music sphering
her ocean of parquet, her stars of spotlights
jingle the silver-chained bracelet that memories her wrist.
Surfing her world, Ms Victory is Ella –
is Bessie –
is Nina –
is Billie –

Kabba Questions the Ontology of Representation, the Catch 22 for 'Black' Writers . . .

Vy giv my boy
dis freebie of a silky blue
    GCSE antology with its three poets
        from three parts of Briten – yor HBC

of Eaney, Blake,
Clarke, showing us how
    to tink and feel? For Part 2, us
        as a bunch of Gunga Dins ju group, *'Poems*

from Udder Cultures
and Traditions'. *'Udder'* is all
    vee are to yoo, to dis cuntry –
        'Udder'? To my son's kabbadi posseee, alll

        yor poets are *'Udder'*!

Vut free-minding teecher
are yoo to luv 'our' poem
    ver a goat's neck is cut for blessing
        new house. 'Our' bastard poet saying such houses

same as Dachau.
My boy, vil he tink ebry new
    Barrett-home muslim hav goat blood-party
        barbeque? All vee do yoo tink is pray for di curse

of incarnations
as in dat scorpion stinging
    'poem', ver di mudder is mantra'd to death?
        Dat writer not know vee hav doctors and rocket

      rickshaw amblance?

Yoo teachers are like
dis Dalgit-Bulram mickeying
    of me as Kabba. I say for di garment
        of my voice may be sestina, sonnet, tanka,

tum-ti-tum
wid best vurds please! A dictation
    of the vay I lecture Punjabi to my boy
        after school. So vut di coconut do – too shy to uze

his voice, he plot me
as 'funny', or a type, even vurse –
    so hee is uzed in British antologies –
        he hide in dis whitey 'fantum' English, blacked,

    to make me sound 'poreign'!

Consummation

Clunks the Chubb lock. With purple
nails and henna soles she softs
the parquet of lemon petals, snuffs
sandalwood to pass the stacked
kettle-and-cutlery gifts, the trunk
unbodying her suits. She peels from
her sari then from her skin she spills
bleached under the 100w light
as the pang of jewellery ignites.
As rehearsed – holds. This once,
she'll tilt along the bolstered vein
of the mattress. She lids her eyes.
A fly nibbles her palm. Played
her part only to be blanked again

by this man who once checked with blast
then signed for her at Passport Control. Who,
against the sponge of the velour headboard
in a double-breasted suit, is holed crumpily,
whose neck and wrists spun in mustard gold.
Dome of pink turban. And pressed-in eyes
that flight their insect ascent only to sprawl over
festoon-bolted velvet curtains. Whose closest family
downstairs, lost in years, with night barely
begun – wolfing to their dance of thuds, as
he lightens the ring-fingered hold on the Holsten,
holding on the last of the warm flat drink

Informant

i have been sitting here
recording myself telling on myself

whatever voice i put on
i know i'm heading for bother

mostly the confessions
i play back to myself

inside my bad-weathered room
are so unrewarding

i may have to go
back into hiding

My Father's Dream of Return

Booming the clouded mountains,
hurtling around and downwards –
the bird-like, plane-like jet
descent of his car speckling
the slant of goats, fast-brake
at the ceremonial elephants,
downwards for the cows mothering
on the plain, fourth gear
he hooters leathery skin
that climbs on husky trees,
some hands fanned into waves
from sunflower fields, some twisted
heads from the sugarcane. Soothing
his engine by the cesspool,
air-conditioned, he awaits
his audience.

My father then imagines
his old village as a ghost
home with its doors padlocked
creaking for the landlord profiting
abroad, yet men are stooped
to the point of his burgundy loafers,
with the old, in the dust who launch
prayers to ascend their stares
from the gold hooping him.
He raises the boot of his Ambassador –
nectars children with boxes
of chum-chums, or cool
sherbets in plastic pipes,

shares out tubs of powder
paints and gunned rainbow
liquids, and elastic party hats.
My father dreams of scattering
fireworks through the sun
on everyone!

I'm plonked on his overall'd knee
catching at scabs of cement
on his breast pocket after his return
from work, as he pictures his built
frame in pinstripes, with voice
blaster than the temple speakers
he'd summon them all to my
wedding with an alabastered
family we'd keep company.
He'd tell them we live over there –
on top of the married mountains
sipping mauve faludas, as we size up
queues of customers (side
by side, in the forecourt shade)
to our almighty BP
stop!

University

On the settling of birds, this man blesses

    his daughter.

She'll split fast for Paddington, then slide

    east

which may as well be the black beyond

    of Calcutta.

The low long curving train opening its

    mouth

gulps from his hands her bags to a far-side

    seat.

He gawps from his thin-rivered, working

    town.

The train roars, the tracks beyond humped

    with light.

The rucksack'd man with whom her eyes

    meet . . .

Five birds pluck their wings off the train

    and fly.

All We Smiley Blacks!

The orient sun zaps us out of our suburban sepia
for the revamped brownfield where the snip red ribbon
disarms our badly lumped blacks, *Cum sheltah in heeya!*
booms the Parky who salutes the Mayor then summons
rockets of confetti parachuting on our regiments of speakers,
tricksters, clowns, crowds, drummers and strummers,
shores of us streaming through the gates in our native gears.

Bullets of light phosphor the applauding leaves
and inspect the plastic petticoat parade of saplings
as the grass lets go with a to-and-fro of Mexican waves
for masked children who kick from orange and cherry swings
diving with some in the spongy sand-pit for hide and seek,
all leaders improvise with a massive khaki ground-sheet
so we may feast on our picnic of chapattis and patties and teas.

A humble-looking man splits a bomb-shaped chum-chum
(leaking its syrup) with a low-caste smiling woman,
an ordinary drowns his lover with almondy puffs
through dandelion clocks that fluff her thread of buttons.
The Parky, with his totem-wand at the heavens, boots up
a stark of clouds. They outline nations of the globe, so
that sky is a screen on which world is mapped . . .
His wand now joins each nation . . . World a flown

pink commingling of clouds on our patch in Slough
whirling so we wage the graft of countries at once.
Sphere'd birds disperse for smithereen air shows
platooning through the cumulus-kissing continents

as butterflies aspire to kaleidoscope the sky,
gaping – we gasp on gases of air that blast
the darkest hunted reaches of our afeard hearts.

One of us juggling skittles, at the flush of this oceanless
borderless, hugging a tree, is a stone's throw away
from our ancestors: *Every day, just there, in Africa!*
One of us blesses, *We're everywhere, welcome to stay!*
One of us, swarthily: *Is dat cloud for England and India?*
Is the stamp of our arrival, our passport this park?
This hologram of home! We holler the flag of our dance!

Singh Song!

I run just one ov my daddy's shops
from 9 o'clock to 9 o'clock
and he vunt me not to hav a break
but ven nobody in, I do di lock –

cos up di stairs is my newly bride
vee share in chapatti
vee share in di chutney
after vee hav made luv
like vee rowing through Putney –

Ven I return vid my pinnie untied
di shoppers always point and cry:
Hey Singh, ver yoo bin?
Yor lemons are limes
yor bananas are plantain,
dis dirty little floor need a little bit of mop
in di worst Indian shop
on di whole Indian road –

Above my head high heel tap di ground
as my vife on di web is playing wid di mouse
ven she netting two cat on her Sikh lover site
she book dem for di meat at di cheese ov her price –

my bride
        she effing at my mum
        in all di colours of Punjabi
        den stumble like a drunk
        making fun at my daddy

my bride
     tiny eyes ov a gun
     and di tummy ov a teddy

my bride
     she hav a red crew cut
     and she wear a Tartan sari
     a donkey jacket and some pumps
     on di squeak ov di girls dat are pinching my sweeties –

Ven I return from di tickle ov my bride
di shoppers always point and cry:
Hey Singh, ver yoo bin?
Di milk is out ov date
and di bread is alvays stale,
di tings yoo hav on offer yoo hav never got in stock
in di worst Indian shop
on di whole Indian road –

Late in di midnight hour
ven yoo shoppers are wrap up quiet
ven di precinct is concrete-cool
vee cum down whispering stairs
and sit on my silver stool,
from behind di chocolate bars
vee stare past di half-price window signs
at di beaches ov di UK in di brightey moon –

from di stool each night she say,
     How much do yoo charge for dat moon baby?

from di stool each night I say,
     Is half di cost ov yoo baby,

from di stool each night she say,
    How much does dat come to baby?

from di stool each night I say,
    Is priceless baby –

Punjabi to Ungreji Guide

buk-buk-buk – prattle

chum-chum – lusciously syrup-hearted, spherically challenged spongy delight enrobed in coconut shavings. Chum-chums hit the spectrum for colours – they can be pink, luminous green, umber, amber, vermilion, etc.

faluda – milkshake with vermicelli

fut-a-fut – instantly

gora – white English male

Holi – festival of colours

jaldi-jaldi – fut-a-fut

jameen – ground beneath your feet

5Ks – symbols of the Sikh religion: kirpan (blade), kara (bangle), kesh (barnet), kacha (boxers) and kunga (brush)

ladoo – saffron-coloured sweetmeats about the size of a golf ball, not as compelling as chum-chums

roti – colloquialism for 'dinnertime'

Rub – GOD!

saathi – lifelong companion

shokri – flirty or, indeed, wanton woman

shrubby – pissed

Ungreji – English

Wahay Guru – exclamatory shot at praising the ten Gurus (used for prayer, mantra, salutation, exclamation, irony, improvisation starter, etc.)